# Guaranteed Victory!

*Now thanks be unto God, which always causeth us to triumph in Christ,*
*and maketh manifest the savour of His knowledge by us in every place.*
— 2 Corinthians 2:14 (KJV)

Bishop Gerald A. Anderson, Sr.

# Guaranteed Victory!

*Now thanks be unto God, which always causeth us to triumph in Christ,*
*and maketh manifest the savour of His knowledge by us in every place.*
— 2 Corinthians 2:14 (KJV)

ISBN: 979-8-9990104-0-7

Scriptures are from the King James Version of the Bible, unless otherwise noted.

# DEDICATON

To my lovely wife,

Thank you for believing in me, praying for me, and always pushing me to be better. Your unwavering support and loving me through it all made this possible every step of the way.

To my five beautiful children —

**Gerald, Jr., Victoria, Valencia, Joshua, and Verneisha** you are my greatest blessings and my daily inspiration.

And to all of my precious grandchildren —

may you always know the strength, faith, and victory that lives within you.

This is for you.

# MY GREATEST BLESSINGS

From left to right (top row): Gerald Jr., Victoria (Rosie), Valencia. Bottom row (left to right): Joshua, Verneisha (Nene).

# TABLE OF CONTENTS

# FORWARD

As the wife of Bishop Gerald A. Anderson, Sr., it is both an honor and a privilege to reflect on the powerful journey that is laid out within these pages. His story, woven through this book, speaks not only to his resilience but to the undeniable truth that when God has called you, no demon from hell can stop you!

From the very beginning, my husband's life has been a testament to God's faithfulness. His unwavering commitment to the call of ministry and the work of the Kingdom has echoed loudly through every trial and triumph. As his biggest supporter, I've witnessed firsthand the obstacles, detours, setbacks, and moments of embarrassment, and even betrayal that have come our way—moments that may have caused others to falter, but never my husband. He stood firm, knowing that God's hand was on his life and that with God, victory was certain.

This book serves as a reminder to all of us: When God has a plan for you, nothing can hinder it. The road may be long, difficult, and filled with challenges, but you are still moving forward. The victory is already secured in Christ. Even when the path is unclear,

God is always working behind the scenes to bring us through to victory.

Through every storm, every struggle, and every test, my husband has emerged victorious because he has kept his eyes on God and remained faithful to the calling. The victory is guaranteed in Christ.

May this book encourage you, strengthen your faith, and remind you that no matter what you face, God has already made a way for you to triumph. Victory in Christ is assured—always.

Love you, Bae.

— Dr. Kim Anderson

# INTRODUCTION

Many times, it's hard to believe that you're winning — especially when life looks nothing like what you prayed for. You've done all the right things. You went to school, earned the degree, put in the work, stayed faithful… but the doors still haven't opened. You're still unemployed. You're still waiting. You're still wondering, *"God, where is the victory in this?"*

You trained your children in the way they should go, just like the Word says. You spoke the promises over them. You raised them in church. But now they're grown — and nowhere near the house of God. You watch them live in ways you never taught, wondering if anything you planted actually took root.

You married in what you believed was the will of God. You sought His face, waited on His timing, did it "right." But now you find yourself divorced — carrying the weight of broken promises and silent prayers. You ask yourself, *"How did it still fall apart if God was in it?"*

These are the moments when the word "victory" feels almost offensive. Because if this is winning, what does losing look like?

I get it. It's one thing to believe in victory when everything is going right. But what about when it's not? What about when your heart is breaking and your faith is tired? When you've done all you could — and still feel like you're losing?

That's where real faith lives.

But even there, God speaks something powerful over your life:

*"Now thanks be unto God, which always causeth us to triumph in Christ..."* (2 Corinthians 2:14)

Not sometimes. **Always.**

Even when it doesn't feel like it.

Even when your hands are empty, your heart is heavy, and your plans are shattered.

This book is for the one who has done everything they knew to do… and still ended up broken. For the one who's holding on to God with one hand and wiping tears with the other. You are not forgotten. You are not forsaken. And no matter what life looks like right now — you are not losing.

*Guaranteed Victory* isn't about perfect endings or instant results. It's about a God who never loses — and because you're in

Him, neither will you. Victory is not a feeling. It's a promise. And in Christ, it's guaranteed.

# GROWING UP IN THE WINDY CITY

I was born on August 8, 1967, at Roseland Hospital in Chicago, Illinois, where the energy of city life blended with the close-knit bonds of family and community. My parents, the late Esau Jr. and Sarah Louise Anderson, were hardworking and deeply proud. They raised me in a lively, bustling home that was anything but ordinary. As the sixth of eleven children, I had a unique upbringing, and being a twin made it even more special—my twin sister and I were often inseparable, like two peas in a pod. My mother told me that we often had visitors who came by just to see us twins.

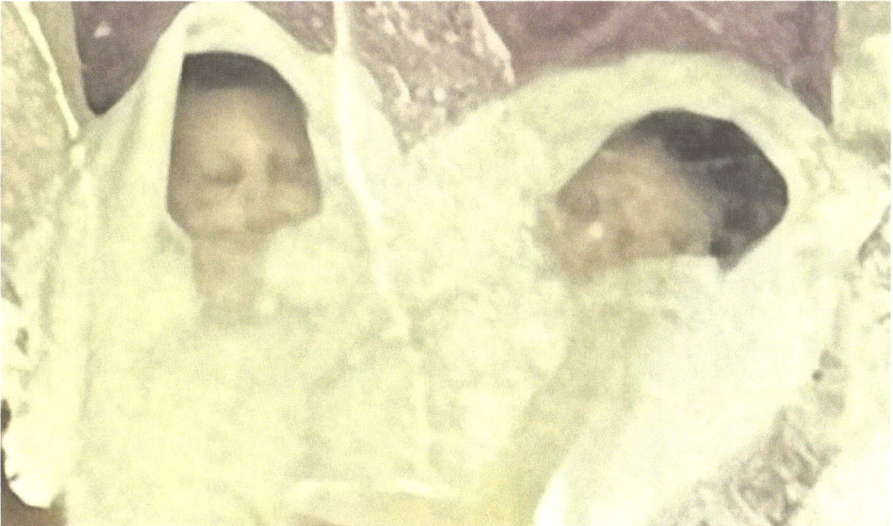

# CHICAGO IS FAMOUSLY KNOWN AS *THE WINDY CITY*

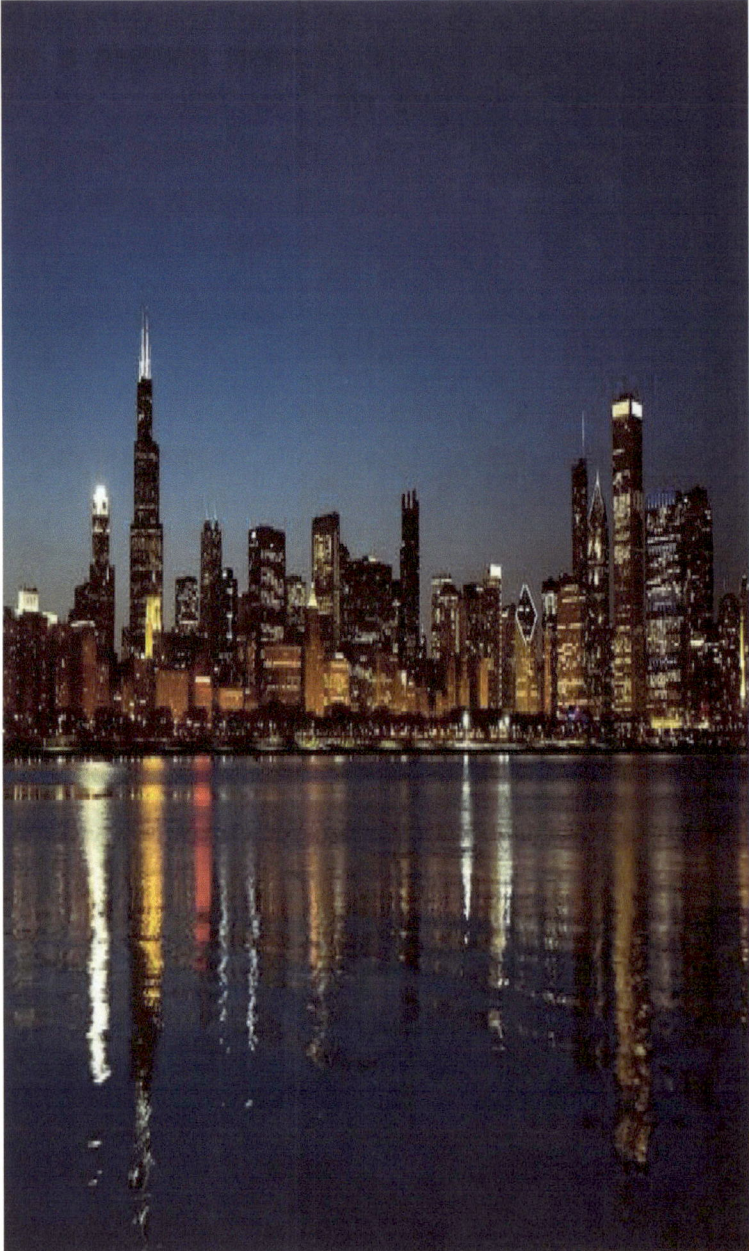

(Jones, 2024)

# ALTGELD GARDENS — THE HEART OF THE CITY, THE SOUL OF A COMMUNITY

I was raised in Altgeld Gardens, one of Chicago's most well-known public housing projects. The Gardens, as we called it, was a world all its own, tucked away on the city's far south side. To many, Altgeld Gardens was synonymous with struggle—the struggle for decent housing, for jobs, for education, for opportunity. But to me, it was home. It was where I learned about the grit of survival, the strength of community, and, most importantly, the resilience of the human spirit.

(WBEZ Chicago Curious City, n.d.)

While I share a bond with all my siblings, I feel especially close to one of my older brothers, Carl Maurice. He was always a sharp dresser and would offer me tips on how to match my ties and dress well as a young boy. Carl and I traveled together to national conventions, shared hotel rooms, and even as I began my ministry, he was always there with advice and guidance. There was nothing he wouldn't do for me. I often think back to when I was being elevated to the office of Bishop in Charlotte, NC. I had no idea that Carl and my sister-in-law, Lorraine Anderson would drive hundreds of miles just to be there and support me. Their presence and support meant the world to me.

Growing up in a family of 11 siblings, life was often tough, and my parents faced constant challenges in making ends meet. My mother, who was on welfare for a time, taught me the value of hard work. As a result, I learned how to cut grass, shovel snow, and even collect pop bottles for spare change. I also worked at a barber shop to help support the family.

There were days when we couldn't wait to get to school because we didn't have food at home. Some mornings, we walked to school just to have a meal. But somehow, the Lord always provided,

4

and my mother would find a way to put dinner on the table. We often had to share clothes, and as a young boy, I wore my older brothers' shoes, pants, and shirts.

Although we were some of the poorest kids around, those times were also some of the best days of my life. Despite the hardships, we learned how to make our own fun. We didn't have bikes like other kids, but we found wood and old wheels to make our own go-carts. We'd head into the woods to build tree houses. I have vivid memories of swinging from tree to tree on a rope, feeling like we were on top of the world.

So, while growing up poor had its challenges, it also gave me a sense of resilience and creativity that I carry with me to this day.

My mother was an incredibly strong, courageous woman who loved the Lord with all her heart. She was a devoted, saved woman of God who cherished her husband and children. Through her actions, she taught us the importance of living righteously, praying, and always putting God first.

As a young boy, I witnessed the struggles my mom faced to make sure we had what we needed. She did everything she could working tirelessly to support us. Even though my father was in the home, he struggled with drugs and alcohol, even though he was fortunate to have good jobs. He would work just enough to get paid, but then squander the money on drugs, alcohol, and gambling. Even though he had his struggles, I still believe he was a family man at heart. My dad would often encourage me to grow up to be a man who loves and takes care of his family.

I was overwhelmed with joy when he came out to support me at my basketball games or visited my church to hear me minister the Word. Believe it or not, before he passed, he became a member of my church. It was truly an honor to eulogize my father when he passed. Getting back to my mother, there was no sacrifice she wasn't willing to make to meet our needs.

One of the greatest blessings my mother received was being able to save enough money to purchase a home, which moved us out of the projects in 1989. It was an overwhelming joy for our family to see her accomplish this dream—she was so proud of that home she had chosen and worked so hard for. Not to mention, after raising all eleven of her children she went back to school and became a Licensed Practical Nurse.

Sadly, on May 1, 1996, my mother passed away, and that day remains one of the hardest of my life. She never had the chance to see me become a pastor, a role she often asked me about with anticipation. Despite her passing, her love, sacrifices, and teachings continue to guide me every day. I can never fully express how much her strength and faith have shaped who I am today.

## IN LOVING MEMORY

In loving memory of my parents, Sarah Louise Anderson and Esau Anderson, whose love, wisdom, and sacrifices shaped the person I am today.

# THE FIRST CUT: HOW 8TH GRADE SHAPED MY FUTURE

As I grew older, I developed a love for basketball in 8th grade. I tried out for the school team, but unfortunately, I didn't make the cut. My coach told me that I was the best player during tryouts, but my behavior got in the way. I was always in trouble, often acting as the class clown. I'd make spitballs and throw them at the backs of my classmates' heads, always finding ways to make people laugh. As a result, I was frequently sent to the principal's office—sometimes daily, sometimes every other day.

Looking back, I remember my coach telling me I had great potential, but he couldn't put me on the team because of my poor behavior. He told me to "get my act together," and that moment was a turning point for me. I realized that my coach saw something in me that I hadn't yet recognized: potential. His words stuck with me, and I made up my mind to change.

# MILESTONES TOGETHER

Celebrating our 8th grade graduation — still side by side, just like always. With my twin sister, Toni — the world knew us simply as 'the twins.'

# THE ROAD TO REDEMPTION

After graduating from 8th grade, I tried out for the freshman basketball team and made it. Making the team was a life-changing moment for me. I went from being the class troublemaker to being focused both in class and on the basketball court. I even earned the nickname "Uweblab," after a former professional basketball player for Indiana University. I had the privilege of playing alongside some great teammates, including NBA star Tim Holloway, Wade "Jamming" Jenkins, Caleb Davis, and Daryl Morgan. During preseason, former NBA player Terry Commins would practice with us, which was an amazing experience.

As my focus shifted, I began to earn the respect of my teachers and principals. My behavior improved significantly, although there was one incident—a fistfight in defense of my sister. Aside from that, I started to gain favor with those around me.

# THE GIFT OF OPPORTUNITY: HOW A SCHOLARSHIP OPENED DOORS

By my senior year of high school, my hard work paid off. I received a scholarship to attend Philander Smith College, an all-Black college in Little Rock, Arkansas. While I was there, I had the honor of meeting Bishop Leodies Warren, the pastor of Christ Temple Church, and his wife Goldie Warren. I was blessed to stay in their home for several months, where I experienced a level of hospitality I'd never known before. Bishop Warren had a private maid who cooked three hot meals a day, and I'll never forget waking up to the smell of fried chicken, eggs, and grits.

However, my time in Arkansas was cut short when I was assaulted by the basketball coach, but I was legally compensated for the incident.

# BACK WHERE IT ALL BEGAN: A RETURN TO HOME AND PURPOSE

In 1987, after returning home to Chicago, I began working at Old Republic Life Insurance in the warehouse. It was during this time that I met Victoria Hamilton at the Indiana Pentecostal Church of God. We married in 1989 and were blessed with five beautiful children. We remained married for 26 years, but unfortunately, our marriage ended in divorce.

Later, I was fortunate to be hired by the Chicago Transit Authority (CTA). While working at the CTA, my focus began to shift more toward ministry. On August 27, 1989, the late Bishop Charles E. Davis officially released me into the ministry. I can still remember the excitement of preaching my first sermon, titled "Plan for Departure." At 21 years old, I was filled with a sense of purpose, especially as I saw my mother, the late Sarah Louise Anderson, in the audience, praising God. That moment solidified for me that God had placed a divine calling on my life.

Throughout my journey, I was guided by the belief that God had a greater plan for me. It was during this time that I fully accepted my calling into ministry, which has shaped much of my life since.

The sacred journey took a significant turn when the late Bishop Arthur M. Brazier anointed my head with oil, affirming the call that God had placed on my life. From that moment, I have walked in faith, trusting God's direction every step of the way.

I was so humbled and honored to be elevated and anointed to the office of District Elder. It was more than a title—it was a divine assignment. I give God all the glory for His grace and faithfulness, and I remain committed to serving His people with integrity, humility, and love.

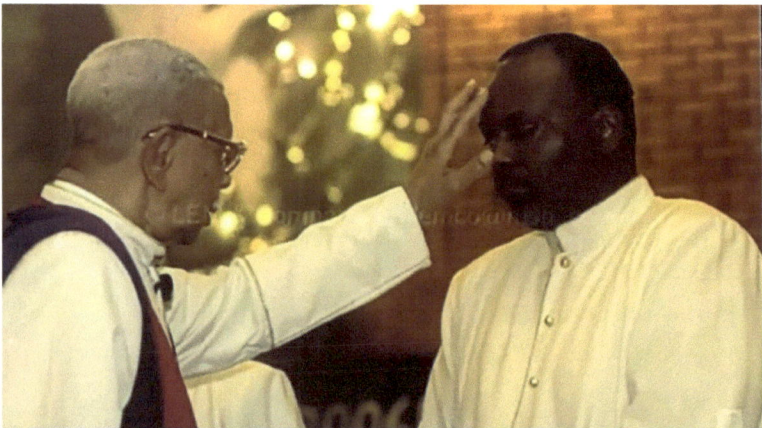

# THE COST OF PRIORITIES

At the age of 21, I was incredibly focused on ministry. However, as the years passed and I began raising a family, the demands of life quickly took over. Having child after child brought many challenges, especially when it came to providing for them. I believed strongly in my role as the provider, and within seven years, I found myself parenting five children with a decent income. While this was a blessing, it was also incredibly challenging because I always wanted my children to have the best.

But the ministry also required my attention. In retrospect, I realized that I was prioritizing ministry over my family, and in doing so, I was neglecting my family in important ways. This is a key point I want to share in this book: while ministry is vital, family is much more important. I put the ministry before my marriage and children, which led to neglect in areas that really mattered.

As the provider, I ensured there was food on the table, and the bills were paid, but I often failed to spend quality, one-on-one time with my children. Intimacy, the kind they longed for, like father-daughter dates or father-son outings, was something I could have done more of. I did a lot, but part of me feels that I could have done so much more. Instead, I focused more on the ministry because I believed it was a divine calling.

Unfortunately, this misplaced priority led to many roadblocks and difficult times in my life. One thing I noticed was that many pastors and bishops placed ministry first, often making their wives and children second. It took me a long time to learn, though, that even with a divine calling, it is imperative to never neglect the structure of your family.

I remember a time when my ex-wife told me that I had taken her youth. She expressed how I was always at church, always serving, and how we never had enough vacations or quality time together as a family. Everything revolved around the church. We were going to church five days a week, and as much as I believed in the importance of attending church, I came to realize that I had made it my singular focus. Church, church, church – and that left little space for my role as a husband and father.

There were times when I was away at preaching revivals and didn't give my children and family the attention they needed because

I thought I was fulfilling my duty by providing financially. There were times I took my kids to church all day on Sunday and would fuss at them about their grades or their focus on studies, not realizing that the constant church attendance was a huge distraction.

Looking back, I also see that I was attending to other people's families before tending to my own. Before I became a pastor, I spent a lot of time assisting my own pastor—driving him around, meeting him at conferences—all while I should have been giving that same time to my ex-wife and children.

Eventually, I became so immersed in the cycle of church, ministry, and serving my pastor that I was elected to serve as the Youth State Young People Chairman over the state of Illinois for the Pentecostal Assemblies of the World (P.A.W.). This added even more responsibilities and took up even more of my time. The more I pursued ministry, the further I drifted from home, from my ex-wife, and from my children, which only added to the strain.

As I continued in ministry, I found myself constantly on the move, running revivals and overseeing nearly 100 churches in Illinois as the youth leader. I was also responsible for organizing quarterly councils and the annual youth convention. The demands of ministry became overwhelming, and in the midst of it all, I stopped working a 9 to 5 job, deciding to dedicate myself full-time to the work of the ministry. I believed this was what God wanted me to do, that it was my divine calling, but the reality was that it came at the cost of my family.

The late Bishop John F. Morris invited me to preach a revival at his church. Around the same time, Bishop Isaac Jackson offered me the opportunity to pastor a church in Mount Vernon, New York, as he was returning to Birmingham, Alabama to pastor his father's church. However, I declined both offers because I did not feel that was God's will at the time. I then traveled to Rome, Georgia to preach for Bishop Nealon Guthrie, who also offered me a church in his council. Again, I declined.

But during a three-day revival at Bethel Apostolic Church of Christ, under the leadership of Bishop Morris, everything changed. On the second night of the revival, while preaching about the year King Uzziah died, I experienced something profound. As I was speaking, I heard a voice in my spirit say, "This is where I want you." I fought the voice, even saying within myself, "No, no, no," as I continued preaching. But by the end of the service, I was overwhelmed with a sense of God's call and came to the submission of His will. I spoke with Bishop Morris afterward and told him I would consider becoming a candidate to take over the church.

A few weeks later, an election was held, and in 1999, I became the pastor of Bethel Apostolic Church of Christ, which is now known as Greater Bethel Apostolic Church of God.

Now, in addition to being the state youth leader, evangelizing full-time, and serving my pastor, I was also pastoring a church. My time was stretched thin, and I continued to prioritize providing for my family, thinking that as long as I paid the bills and kept food on the table, I was being a good husband and father.

But looking back, I see the mistake I made: while I had a divine calling, I had neglected to prioritize my spouse and children. Ministry is important, but God does not want us to neglect the people closest to us. Our spouse and children are a priority. We must ensure that they are never neglected, even when we are called to ministry.

**A healthy relationship with our spouse and family is foundational to a healthy ministry.** You can serve and minister to others, but if you neglect the ones who matter most to you—your spouse and children—then you risk damaging the very foundation of your life. After all, your spouse and children need ministry the most.

# STEPPING INTO MY CALLING

"Stepping into the calling God had ordained – installed as pastor, 1999"

# THE LORD'S DOING

"This is the Lord's doing; it is marvellous in our eyes." — Psalm 118:23

# THE REALITIES OF MINISTRY

Let me return to talking about the church. Growing up in the ministry, I had a certain idea of how things were supposed to be. However, as I grew closer to God and matured in my faith, I began to realize that much of what I had assumed about ministry wasn't exactly what I thought. I served in many capacities in the church—cleaning, going down to clean up after floods, helping to build a new church, raising money by selling candy, playing the drums, driving the church van, teaching in the Sunday School department, participating in Christmas and Easter plays, cleaning the kitchen, and so much more. I even served as the pastor's armor bearer. My hands were full in ministry, and despite the ups and downs, the mistakes I made, and the challenges I faced, I thought serving in the ministry was very rewarding.

But over time, I came to understand that only God can truly reward us for our service. Let's talk for a minute about what I discovered in my journey. As I became more involved in church ministry, I realized that things were not always as they seemed. I noticed that many people weren't who they appeared to be, and the more God used me, the more I faced resentment. Jealousy began to creep in, and I saw how people in higher places in the ministry would influence my pastor against me. I began to experience opposition— even from my pastor—during my time in ministry. At first, I couldn't understand why this was happening, but eventually, I learned the reason behind it.

This opposition put a wedge between me and my pastor. We had been close, and I understood him well, so I could detect when something wasn't right. As time passed, I continued to serve him faithfully, but I began to notice how others would speak to him and cause him to act differently. I remember one particular time when I sat down with my pastor and expressed my desire to serve him full-time. He seemed supportive at first and told me that he would need time to think about it. On three separate occasions, he brought up the idea of making me full-time, but during the third meeting, he called in the administrator. She stated, "Well, Bishop, we're not able to hire anyone full-time." It was a discouraging blow, especially since I had been giving so much of myself to serve him and still taking care of my family.

To make matters worse, just two weeks later, the church hired someone else full-time. I went to speak with my pastor about it, and his response was, "It wasn't me; it was the administrator." Though I was discouraged, I continued to serve faithfully. But at that point, my eyes were opening to the reality of how things operate in ministry. I had always focused on the spiritual and ministerial aspects, not paying much attention to the business side of things.

As time went on, I grew more mature, both in my relationship with God and in my understanding of ministry. I began to recognize that the opposition I faced was actually a sign that God's hand was on me, preparing me for something greater. I realized that everything I was doing in ministry—no matter the challenges—was for the glory of God, not for man. My mother had always taught me to love and respect the church, and I carried that with me in everything I did, knowing that it was ultimately for God's glory.

However, I also began to see things in the ministry that were not pleasing to God. There were mistakes I made, decisions I made in the name of ministry that I now understand were not in alignment with God's will. I observed, took heed, and learned from those experiences, knowing that when God called me to pastor, I would do my best to avoid those same mistakes and ensure that my leadership was in line with His will.

# NEW BEGINNING: PASTORING GREATER BETHEL

A few months after the situation with my pastor, doors began to open. After much prayer and reflection, I made the decision to accept the calling to become pastor. I spoke to my pastor about the decision, and at that time, he gave me his full blessing. However, despite his initial support, when I officially became the pastor in October of 1999, I went to visit him, and he didn't want to have anything to do with me. Talk about a tough day that was.

Nevertheless, I pressed forward, stepping into the role of pastor at The Greater Bethel Apostolic Church of God. Now, I was full-time in ministry—serving as the pastor, continuing as the state youth leader, and fully committed to the journey God had set before me. The church, located at 717 West Garfield Boulevard in Chicago, IL, was in need of significant work. It was a great challenge, but God's blessings were evident. In my first five years of pastoring, I was able to repair the building and see the membership grow.

While pastoring, I also continued working within the council under the guidance of Bishop Arthur M. Brazier, a great man of God who imparted much wisdom to me as a pastor. On the day of my installation, I was honored to have both my pastor, Bishop Charles E. Davis, and the Honorable Diocesan Bishop Arthur M. Brazier, who installed me as pastor. It was a great honor, though bittersweet, because my mother had passed away and my father did not attend the ceremony. Still, I could feel the presence of the Lord moving in that moment, and I knew He was guiding me.

As time went on, I devoted countless hours to both the church and my role as state youth leader. The church began to grow, and I sensed there was a need for a new location. At that particular time, the Lord blessed me with the opportunity to find a new space. Eager to get advice, I picked up my pastor, the late Bishop Charles E. Davis, to take him to the new location. I wanted his wisdom and insight—not seeking money, but hoping to make him proud of the progress I was making. As we arrived and I showed him the potential, his response was, "Son, you are moving too fast; take it easy."

Although I respected his words, I felt a bit down. I was seeking approval and guidance from my pastor, and I wasn't sure what to make of his cautious response. Still, I decided to take the next step and reach out to the late Bishop Arthur M. Brazier. I asked him what he thought of the idea, and his response was encouraging. He said, "Son, when can you come to my office?" I replied, "I can come tomorrow." So, I set up a meeting, took pictures of the church, and shared my plans with him.

When I showed Bishop Brazier the pictures and explained my intent, he said, "Oh, I think this is a great idea. What can I do to help you?" I was taken aback and thought to myself, "Wow, this must be the hand of God." Bishop Brazier not only gave me his blessing but also connected me to the right person at the bank to secure the finances needed to seal the deal.

I want to emphasize that we did not ask any pastors, bishops, or anyone for funding; God provided everything. I'll never forget what my pastor, Bishop Davis, had told me: that I wouldn't get $20 for the church when I sell it lol. But by God's grace, I sold the church for $176,000. On the day of the closing, which was in 2004, I went back to show my pastor the check. When he saw it, he said, "The Lord must be with you, son." Those words meant so much to me, especially because he had always shown me tough love.

Two days later, the Lord blessed me to close on the new location. But when we got to the closing, we were surprised to receive $71,000 back. We used that surplus as the initial down payment for renovations at the new location.

Today, we worship at 2122 W. 79th Street, Chicago, IL, and I am continually humbled by the journey and the blessings God has poured out on us.

# Greater Bethel Apostolic Church of God

2122 W. 79th Street
Chicago, IL 60620

## IN THE MIDST OF OPPOSITION: A PASTOR'S PATH

Now that we were in the new location, we began to see the Lord move in a mighty and special way. The membership grew, and I was blessed to be broadcasting on 1570 AM radio and on television at WJYS, Channel 62, here in Chicago, IL. While we experienced God's hand in incredible ways, there was still opposition.

One of the most significant moments in my ministry came when I felt led to run for council chairman. My pastor, Bishop Charles E. Davis, had become the diocesan bishop of the state of Illinois for the Pentecostal Assemblies of the World, and I thought this would be a great opportunity to step into a leadership role. I believed I was well-loved and accepted in the church, and that this would be a seamless transition. However, I was blindsided by the reality that the church, like the world, operated in its own form of politics.

I didn't realize at the time that there were behind-the-scenes efforts to prevent me from winning the council chairman seat. As the week of the election arrived, I felt optimistic—many people had given me positive feedback, saying things like, "We're looking forward to you being our next council chairman." The atmosphere was charged with excitement, and I was hopeful.

During the business session on Friday, the announcement was made. Over 800 people were present, eagerly awaiting the outcome. When they announced the winner, the room fell completely silent. It was so quiet you could hear a pin drop. The shock was palpable. Several people came up to me afterward, saying, "Pastor Anderson, I don't understand what happened." I, too, was confused and disheartened.

Despite my feelings of discouragement, I praised the Lord with my pastor and shared with him, "Something isn't right." His response was, "Son, I don't know what happened." The loss was disheartening, and it took a toll on my spirit.

A month later, my older brother, who was a part of my ministry, decided to write a letter of dissatisfaction about the election to Diocesan Bishop Charles E. Davis and the presiding bishop at the time, Bishop Horace E. Smith. This letter sparked an uproar in the Illinois District Council, leading to tensions among the pastors and creating a significant wedge between me and my pastor, Bishop Davis, due to the way the election had played out.

This resulted in an executive board meeting with the pastors, Bishop Davis's wife, and myself included, in my role as District Elder, to address the election process because I have always felt that there was a conflict of interest. I've always believed there was a clear conflict of interest in that election, considering she was both the bishop's wife and the mother of one of the candidates. She was involved in several aspects of the election process, and on more than one occasion, I personally witnessed her in roles that raised serious questions about impartiality — not to mention, the ballot box itself was kept in her office.

During this meeting, it was revealed that 200 ballots had been omitted by the ballot committee. This discovery caused a stir, and it was a challenging moment for everyone involved. I vividly remember seeing my pastor with his head hung low, disheartened by the situation.

In that moment, I raised my hand, and Bishop Davis acknowledged me to speak. I made a motion to accept the election outcome, regardless of the omitted ballots, and to move forward in unity. It was a difficult decision, but I knew it was necessary for the peace and progression of the council.

After losing the election, Bishop Charles E. Davis graciously invited me to preach at my home church, which is also his church on a Sunday morning. While I was grateful for the opportunity, the experience came with a painful moment. His wife at the time confronted me in the hallway and said, 'If you were my son, I would slap you in the face.' I believe she said this out of frustration, stemming from the allegations and the tension surrounding what had taken place in the meeting. Bishop Davis happened to step into the hallway and quickly intervened, saying, 'Girl, leave him alone,' and diffused the moment. She then responded, 'Oh, give me a hug.' It's moments like these that teach you how to respond with grace and manage opposition when it arises — often unexpectedly — in life.

# A HIGHER CALLING: OVERCOMING OPPOSITION TO STEP INTO PURPOSE

At the time, it seemed like a setback in my ministry, but little did I know, the Lord was preparing me for something greater. I remained faithful to the organization I served, continuing to support my pastor and bishop for another four years until it was time to move on. Along the way, I faced many challenges, but as I reflect on those moments, I realize that the Lord was using them to prepare me for the call He had placed on my life.

In 2012, I was sitting down for breakfast, and across from me was a group of pastors enjoying their meal. Suddenly, the late Apostle Clifford E. Turner, who had been seated at another table, got up, walked over to mine, and said, "The Lord told me to give you a word: your season is up in the organization you're in. It's time for you to move on. When you move on, new doors will open for you."

At the time, I didn't immediately receive that word. I loved the organization I was a part of, and honestly, I was hesitant to even consider leaving. I thought to myself, *Huh, I don't know about this.*

But little did I know, I was about to face a season of transformation that I wasn't prepared for.

At that moment, I was deeply in debt—1.5 million dollars in the hole—and yet, by faith, I made the decision to take a leap and move on from the organization. To my surprise, the moment I stepped out in obedience, my debt was cut in half. God had already begun to move, and the doors He promised were beginning to open.

On December 31, 2012, the Lord impressed upon me to transition from the Pentecostal Assemblies of the World to the Apostolic Faith Fellowship under the leadership of Presiding Bishop Charles E. Johnson. In 2013, I was elevated to Diocesan Bishop over the states of Illinois, Iowa, Indiana, and Ohio. At that time, everything seemed to be falling into place. I was preaching the Word of God, loved my presiding bishop, and had the privilege of establishing councils. It felt like everything was on track.

However, I've come to understand that whenever the Lord blesses us, He is also preparing us for where He wants to take us next. I didn't realize I would soon face another obstacle—one that was deeply painful and challenged the core of who I was.

I had served faithfully for eight years, but in the last two years of that eight years, rumors began to spread among the bishops and leaders of the fellowship. They falsely claimed that I did not believe in the baptism of Jesus' Name. I was completely unaware that these conversations were taking place, and I was never included in any meetings to address the matter. I had always believed the favor of the Lord was on my life, and the people loved me. The organization had received me with open arms, but I came to realize that politics even existed within the church.

The rumors were painful and hurtful. I approached the presiding bishop about the situation, and his response was, "I know you are apostolic and believe in the baptism of Jesus' Name, just let this die." I felt that was the wrong response. Why should something as critical as this be allowed to simply die when I had never been given a chance to address it? It became clear to me that there was a plot to silence me, fueled by the favor of God on my life.

The inability to resolve this issue left me with deep pain. Then, in 2019, the world was hit by the COVID-19 pandemic. In the midst of my battle with the virus, the Lord spoke to me clearly. While I was sick in bed, He revealed that it was time for me to step into something new. He gave me the name of the organization that would carry my vision: *Jesus Is Lord of the Apostolic Faith Churches International* (J.I.L). During that time, I began to make the necessary preparations for this next phase of my life and ministry.

In July 2020, J.I.L. was officially established, and I was elevated to the role of Presiding Bishop. Looking back, I now understand that the calling on my life was always much greater than I had anticipated. I knew I had a calling, but not to this extent.

Through this journey, I've learned that when God places a calling on your life, it's not always an easy path. Each level brings its own challenges and opposition. As we grow spiritually and move from one level to another, attacks will come. But these challenges are not meant to break us; they are part of God's preparation for the assignment He has given us.

As Matthew 22:14 reminds us, "For many are called, but few are chosen." When God has chosen you for His purpose, you must be ready for opposition. It is through this opposition that God propels us toward our destiny.

## A HISTORICAL GATHERING

JILOAFCI FIRST NATIONAL CONVENTION

# STAYING FOCUSED AND GROUNDED IN THE CALL

So, how do you maintain focus and stay grounded in your calling, especially when faced with trials and opposition? For me, the answer lies in the foundation my mother, the late Sarah Louise Anderson, laid for me. From a young age, she instilled in me the importance of prayer, fasting, and reading the Word of God. These three practices became the pillars that gave me strength and helped me stay focused, even when I wanted to give up.

I believe my mother knew I was called even when I was just a child. She saw something in me that I didn't fully understand at the time. Even as a young kid, I showed signs of leadership that came with a deep sense of responsibility. Looking back over my ministry, I now realize that the heart of a leader was within me from the beginning. It often seemed like I was always catering to others, stepping into various ministries and helping wherever there was a need. At the time, I didn't know that the Lord was using those moments to shape me for leadership.

As a young pastor, I had the privilege of traveling worldwide, and in many of those places, I encountered leaders who would often tell me, "You act like you've been here before, you have so much wisdom." I had no idea how those words would resonate with me later on, but looking back, I can see that the Lord had been preparing me for leadership all along.

Let's delve deeper into an often-overlooked topic: the politics of the church. Many people expect the church to be solely spiritual, but the reality is that it comes with its ups and downs, pros and cons, and complexities. The truth is, the church world can be very political.

As a young boy, I had the opportunity to work in nearly every area of the church, except for pastoring and serving as a deacon. Some of my roles included cleaning the church, playing the drums, teaching Sunday School, serving in the Youth Department, working in the kitchen, driving the church vans, acting as an armor bearer to the pastor, and serving as a local minister—the list goes on.

Through these experiences, I learned an important lesson: in ministry, the higher you rise, the more opposition you encounter. I began to experience roadblocks in ministry, even though I thought everyone shared the same goal. I witnessed how people turned others against my ministry. At one point, I saw individuals of influence speak negatively about me to my pastor, and as a result, he began to treat me differently. What made it especially painful was that he wasn't just my pastor—he was my spiritual father.

Spiritual Father

Bishop Charles E. Davis

In spite of it all, I understood the calling on my life. As a young man, I moved from one level to the next, ultimately leading to pastorship. I remain amazed at how people who preach the Bible and carry the same calling can operate in hatred, jealousy, and envy. Then again, I shouldn't be surprised—the Bible warns us of these things.

And then again, I understand what the Bible says in Zechariah 13:6: *"And one shall say unto him, What are these wounds in thine hands? Then he shall answer, Those with which I was wounded in the house of my friends."* Opposition, while we may think it comes from the world, in fact, often comes from those in the house of the Lord.

As I reflect on these experiences, I want to offer guidance to up-and-coming ministers: if you desire to go where God is taking you, expect to face roadblocks. The enemy does not want you to reach your God-given potential. These challenges are part of the journey and a testament to the strength of your calling. Stay focused on your purpose, trust God, and keep moving forward.

## SPEAKING THROUGH THE STRUGGLE

One of the challenges I faced early in life was a speech problem that made communication, especially pronunciation, difficult—even now in ministry. There have been many occasions, even from family members, when I was mocked for not speaking clearly or for mispronouncing words. But I refused to let that stop me or silence the call on my life. Exodus 4:12 reminds us: *"Now therefore go, and I will be with thy mouth, and teach thee what thou shalt say."*

## A HEART FULLY COMMITTED TO THE LORD

I have reached a point where I've transitioned from simply attending church to embracing a true relationship with God. A relationship, by definition, is a connection through blood or marriage. I realized that when I surrendered my life to the Lord, I experienced a spiritual "blood transfusion."

As a young pastor, I felt a deep sense of dedication and loyalty to the divine calling placed on my life. This isn't something one can wish for or desire—it is a divine order from God. It required a personal commitment from me, one grounded in faith and trust in Him. Psalms

37:5 reminds us: *"Commit thy way unto the Lord; trust also in Him, and He shall bring it to pass."*

My journey has been entirely focused on trusting God's ability to lead and guide me. Everything I've done in life has been aimed at pleasing Him. Proverbs 16:3 emphasizes this: *"Commit thy works unto the Lord, and thy thoughts shall be established."* I am where I am today because the Lord has guided my steps each day.

In ministry, a deep love for both God and His people is essential. Challenges will come—you will be forsaken, mistreated, persecuted, and hurt by others, as I have experienced. But because of the love you have for God, you persevere. Deuteronomy 6:5 commands us: *"Love the Lord your God with all your heart, with all your soul, and with all your strength."* Similarly, Matthew 22:37 teaches: *"You shall love the Lord your God with all your heart, with all your soul, and with all your mind."* This love must be deep and unwavering, compelling us to give God our all.

1 Kings 8:61 (NIV) further instructs: *"And may your hearts be fully committed to the Lord our God, to live by His decrees and obey His commands, as at this time."* In my life, not everything has gone as

I would have liked. There have been many disappointments, but my full commitment to the Lord has kept me steadfast in pursuing the call He has placed on my life.

Here are some key points on how to remain committed to serving God:

1.      Uphold God in your life.

2.      Honor Him in your home.

3.      Reflect Him in your workplace.

4.      Carry His presence into every place you go.

5.      Make God visible in everything you think, say, and do.

Additionally, it's vital to guard your commitment and not allow anyone to deter you from the assignment God has placed on your life. Family members, as much as you love them and they love you, should not interrupt or divert you from your mission, calling, or purpose. Deuteronomy 10:12-13 reminds us: *"And now, Israel, what does the Lord thy God require of thee, but to fear the Lord thy God, to walk in all His ways, and to love Him, and to serve the Lord thy God with all thy heart and with all thy soul, to keep the commandments of the Lord, and His statutes, which I command thee this day for thy good."*

Following Christ often requires great sacrifice, including forsaking all to fulfill His call. Matthew 6:24-25 underscores the importance of full devotion: *"No man can serve two masters, for either he will hate the one and love the other, or else he will hold to the one and despise the other. You cannot serve God and mammon. Therefore I say unto you, take no thought for your life, what you shall eat, or what you shall drink; nor yet for your body, what you shall put on. Is not the life more than meat, and the body more than raiment?"*

This passage reminds us that God's provision is sufficient. Our priority must always be serving Him wholeheartedly, without being divided by worldly concerns or distractions.

We must make our faith real by putting it into action daily. Colossians 3:23-25 says: *"Whatever you do, do it heartily, as to the Lord and not to men, knowing that from the Lord you will receive the reward of the inheritance; for you serve the Lord Christ. But he who does wrong will be repaid for what he has done, and there is no partiality."*

# GOD IS IN CONTROL

So, let me conclude by saying that where I am now is not the final destination of where the Lord is going to take me. Through all the ups and downs, the struggles and triumphs, I am grateful for the blessings in my life—my five beautiful children, Gerald, Jr., Victoria Rose, Valencia, Joshua Emmanuel, and Vernisha along with all of my beautiful grandchildren. The Lord also has blessed me with my wonderful wife, Dr. Kim Anderson and three bonus children, Jonathan, Jessica, and Jasmin. As I reflect on the word 'divine,' I am reminded of the unique purpose and plan God has for my life. I am deeply grateful for the path He has laid before me, knowing that there is so much more ahead. My journey has led me to serve as a Presiding Bishop, overseeing multiple churches across different cities and states. Looking back, I now clearly understand why God led me on the path He did—because to truly care for God's people, one must have the heart of a shepherd. Pastors need a pastor who can relate to the struggles they face, and I, too, have walked through those challenges. So, to everyone reading this book, stay tuned—because God's work in me is far from over."

# THE CALL

From a young age, I sensed there was something greater than myself that I was being drawn toward. I couldn't yet put words to it, but there was a call—deep within my heart—that I could feel even before I understood what it meant. God had a plan for my life, one that would unfold in ways I could never have imagined.

As a child, I remember playing near the train tracks, lost in the moment, when suddenly I heard the distant sound of an oncoming train. I wasn't paying attention, and before I knew it, the train was almost upon me. In a split second, I jumped into a small hole beneath the tracks. I could feel the vibrations of the train as it passed right over my head. Looking back, I know it was only by God's grace that I wasn't killed. He spared my life that day.

There was another time when I found myself in a life-threatening situation. I had been caught stealing tomatoes from someone's garden. As I tried to run, the man, furious with me, fired a shot. Miraculously, the bullet missed. The fear I felt in that moment made me realize how close I had come to losing my life. But more importantly, it reminded me that God had a purpose for me.

Now, looking back, I can see how God's hand was on me, protecting me even when I didn't fully understand what was happening. I realize now that I was being preserved for something greater. Even then, He was preparing me for the call He had on my life.

A call from God doesn't always come with clarity or immediate understanding. Often, it begins as a quiet whisper—a gentle prompting that stirs in your spirit, urging you toward a purpose bigger than yourself. It's a pull that doesn't always make sense at first, but as you walk through life, the pieces start to fall into place.

For me, this call became more apparent as I grew older, through challenges, moments of grace, and experiences that opened my eyes to a greater purpose. Looking back, I can see that even in the moments when I wasn't fully aware of it, God was at work, preparing me for what was ahead. This is the story of how I came to recognize and respond to that call—how it shaped my life and continues to guide me every day.

# GUARANTEED VICTORY

2 Corinthians 2:14 (KJV) states "Now thanks be unto God, which always causeth us to triumph in Christ, and maketh manifest the savour of his knowledge by us in every place."

Psalms 37: 12-13 says *The wicked plotteth against the just, and gnasheth upon him with his teeth. The Lord shall laugh at him: for he seeth that his day is coming.* No matter what's going on around you, remember this: **God laughs at the wicked**. Psalm 37:12–13 reminds us that even when the enemy plots, God is not shaken — because **He already knows how the story ends**. That truth reminds us: the Lord is always on our side. And when God is for you, you cannot lose.

In your walk with God, there will be moments when you feel like giving up — when you want to throw in the towel and quit. But because you carry a divine calling and a divine purpose, God will not let you stay down. He will always allow you to rise above every circumstance. Your victory is guaranteed. So even when it *looks* like you're losing, you're actually winning. Even in your most hopeless moments, your victory remains secure — because God sees your ending before your beginning.

As Paul declared, *"We are more than conquerors through Christ Jesus."* And many of us — pastors, ministers, and believers alike — are still trying to figure out how we've come this far. But we've come to one simple and undeniable conclusion: **It's the hand of God.** He gives provision. He opens doors. He creates new paths. He makes a way where there was no way — and He will continue to make a way for you to fulfill the purpose He has placed on your life

So as I close out this book, I've come to fully embrace this truth: **God is in complete control of our lives.** There is purpose in every moment — even the ones that feel uncertain or overwhelming. **Winning, even when it doesn't look like you're winning — that's what Guaranteed Victory truly means.** It's the assurance that with God, the outcome is already settled in your favor.

**You win.**

**Guaranteed Victory.**

## VICTORY IS ALREADY WON

Today, I realize that in life, there are times when victory feels distant—when challenges seem overwhelming, and the finish line is nowhere in sight. Yet, the truth remains: Victory is already won in Christ. Even when the circumstances do not align with our expectations, and even when the path ahead appears unclear, God's Word assures us that we are more than conquerors through Him who loved us (Romans 8:37).

It's easy to get caught in the struggle and question the outcome, but victory in Christ does not rely on what we see or feel in the moment. God's faithfulness is not dictated by our temporary circumstances. When we are in Christ, victory is not just a possibility—it is a certainty.

# REFERENCES

Jones, M. (2024). The Surprising Reason Why Chicago Is Called the

"Windy City. https://www.rd.com/article/chicago-windy-city/

King James Bible. (2024). King James Bible Online.

https://www.kingjamesbibleonline.org/ (Original work

published 1769).

WBEZ Chicago Curious City (n.d.). The Altgeld Gardens Memorial

Wall is part of Chicago history. But its future is uncertain.

https://www.wbez.org/curious-city/2023/01/27/the-history-

of-the-altgeld-gardens-memorial-wall-in-chicago

www.ingramcontent.com/pod-product-compliance
Lightning Source LLC
Chambersburg PA
CBHW042129080426
42735CB00001B/20